The Impact System™

Becoming a Leader

Achieve Duplication in your business

Howard
Best wishes & to your Success

Stephan Longworth *Jan 12'*

imageplus publishing

imageplus_{publishing}

Published by
Imageplus publishing
PO Box 458,
Macclesfield, Cheshire SK10 2WY
Telephone: +44 (0)845 607 6724
info@imageplus.org.uk
www.imageplus.org.uk

First Edition: 2011 Stephan Longworth
ISBN 978-0-9570506-0-0

Printed in Great Britain by imageplus, Macclesfield

About the author

Stephan Longworth was born and raised on a south Manchester council estate. He had a comprehensive school education, then studied Engineering at Stockport College of Technology. He worked in aviation as a marshaller/airside safety officer and trainer.

Stephan is a student of success, and over the last 17 years has risen steadily to the top in the Network Marketing industry. His driving force is helping others to reach their true potential.

Stephan is currently a National Group Leader with the Utility Warehouse, one of the largest and most successful companies in the Network Marketing industry. He has built a team with in excess of 52,000 customers (at the time of writing), and an annual turnover of tens of millions of pounds a year. He enjoys a lifestyle he once only dreamed of.

He is a respected speaker, with a unique style that not only inspires and motivates his audience, but that also delivers practical tools that help people achieve success.

This is Stephan's first book.

Acknowledgements and dedication

I have gathered the information in this book - unscientifically - over years and years from countless people, countless places. I owe my knowledge and understanding to the advice and insights of many people who have given generously of their time, patience and energy to initiate me into, and educate me in, the mysteries of business, life and this amazing industry of ours; Network Marketing.

I was tutored by some of the best in the business, National Network Leaders Clive Leach and Diana Ross, who have one of the largest, most stable and profitable businesses in the industry. If it wasn't for their driving force and tenacity, I would not be where I am now.

To all the authors, contributors, teachers, friends and acquaintances who have helped me; my thanks.

And, where appropriate; my apologies!

I would also like to thank:

Joan, Joe, Carol, Kieron, Graham, Peter, Paul, Robin, Wes, Jimmy, Gary, Chris, Steve.

The Company executives, the Hon. Charles Wigoder, Andrew Lindsay MBE.

Credits and special thanks to:

Angela Brady-D'Souza; your keen eye was invaluable. Only a dear friend would take the time to read through many rough drafts of this book.

Alan Hamilton from Image Plus publishing, for all your hard work and patience.

Humphrey Couchman, who edited this book. Your editorial skills and knowledge were an invaluable asset to this project. Thank you for your helpful insights and suggestions, thanks for believing in me and in the value of this work.

Finally, thanks to **Wayne Coupland**, for your help and support; not only to myself but the entire network. Your respect for the Distributors in our business is infectious; you are both an inspiration and a friend.

With love, I dedicate this book to:

Dad, Mum, Barrie and **Sam**.

To **Ashley** and **Jamie**, the finest sons anyone could ever hope to have, sons that have been so forgiving over the years, sons whose hearts are bigger than the bodies that carry them... thank you.

And mere thanks cannot express my gratitude to my wife, **Georgia**, for her encouragement, support, love and belief in me. **Georgia**, you have been my oak tree, my rock; I can never fully repay you.

'I have a passion to help team members achieve success in their UWDC business' - Stephan Longworth

"Stephan Longworth is a remarkable leader in the networking industry. When Diane and I first met Stephan it was obvious that he had a massive desire to success. Over the years he has been like a sponge, soaking up ideas, concepts & strategies and has exhibited the work effort to create and build a large, dynamic network of authorised independant distributors. Stephan has never been afraid to ask for help and it has and still is a priviledge to have Stephan and his wife, Georgia, as great colleagues and true friends."

Clive Leach & Diana Ross,

National Network Leaders & Authorised Distributors

Contents

Foreword 8

Part 1 – Get your head right **13**

Attitude 15

Belief 26

Positive thinking 33

Association 38

Leadership 44

Motivation 48

Producing fruit 51

Part 2 – Getting started right **53**

Building a team – leveraging time 55

First steps for the new Distributor 57

Prepare to take action 63

Contacting and Inviting 66

Commitment 82

Different ways to present the business opportunity 85

The follow-up 91

What it takes to succeed 97

Appendix – Suggested reading and listening **101**

Don't quit **103**

Foreword

Dear friend,

Congratulations and welcome!

You might be about to begin a journey towards creating a business of lasting success, a business you truly deserve. You might already be on that journey.

Either way, I have huge respect for what you are doing.

I have been there, and I know how it feels. I joined the Utility Warehouse – or Telecom Plus as it was then – some years ago. No other business in Britain offers everyone such an opportunity to start with nothing but a dream and become financially free. It treats each person with equal respect.

Be mindful that you should be your own best customer. Remember when you bring a new person into your team, to ensure that they get some customers or no one gets paid!

I started, like everyone else does, at the bottom. But with drive, effort and dogged determination, I have climbed our 'stairway to success'.

For several years now, I have been passionately pursuing the answers to these questions: What shapes our behaviour? What shapes our success? How can we create lasting change within ourselves? How can we create lasting change within others?

Through my studies, from seminars, books and CDs, from my mistakes and successes, and from my interaction over the years with an incredibly diverse group of people — from full-time parents to professional athletes, from teachers and trainers to high-ranking police officers, from blue-collar workers to top-flight executives — I have combined tools and strategies which have helped me maximise my capabilities.

I have long envisioned the creation of a system; one where new Distributors can immediately apply themselves and make profound changes in the quality of their lives, by building successful businesses.

And now I feel genuinely excited, passionate and privileged, to have the opportunity to share with you the best of what I have learned.

I call it 'The Impact System™.'

The success of all of our Distributorships is shaped by what we know, what we believe, by our habits and by our skills.

The Impact System™ has given me, and now can give you, the opportunity to take control of these forces, and design your business exactly the way you want it to be. You will acquire the skills, knowledge and strategies necessary to make your ambitions come true.

The Impact System™ can help you take control and change the quality of your business, and your life, forever.

You'll learn methods and techniques that I discovered over many years.

There are many ways to be successful in Network Marketing. But I have found that some ways are better than others. I'd like to share them with you.

And through it all, you will develop the skills you need to become a leader in this business.

Accept the opportunities ahead with enthusiasm, and your business will prosper.

But always remember this; the Impact System™ is built around you taking the simple actions, on a daily basis, that will reward you the most. In business, activity always comes before results. Income follows correct activity.

This business is built on the laws of business, not the laws of the casino. This is not a game of chance. You must understand that there are skills you need to learn to be successful.

My goal in developing the Impact System™ is to provide the best support possible to every Distributor. If you are without immediate upline support, this programme can be the success coach you're looking for.

If you have great upline support, this programme will complement that, and make you better.

I understand that everybody who enters this business has different amounts of time, energy, self-confidence, desire and talent. That's one of the reasons I have made the Impact System™ adaptable to every Distributor, from the novice to the more experienced.

When I designed the Impact System™, I had in mind a Distributor investing one to two hours per day into his or her business. But you can adjust it down, if you have less time to put in, or you can adjust it up, if you have more ambitious goals.

Life produces extraordinary rewards for those who give in extraordinary ways. Let's make a commitment today to participate together with intensity and passion, let's go beyond anything we've done before. Let's start the process of taking our business – and our lives – to the next level. Let's start NOW!

Above all, this book is meant to help the men and women joining this great business; those many thousands of people who still dare to dream big, who believe in enterprise and being their own boss. In these troubled economic times, many have begun to question themselves, and our country. You won't find such fears haunting Utility Warehouse Distributors. We will keep the flame alive when so many others have lost hope.

Believe in the abilities you possess and give yourself the necessary time to get the results you desire.

Start right where you are... but start.

Best wishes, and respect,

Stephan.

PART 1
GET YOUR
HEAD RIGHT

Attitude

Attitude is going to be a major factor in the success or failure of your business.

Your attitude is your fuel.

A positive mental attitude is about not living in a fantasy world, but facing reality; with anticipation, not apprehension.

What you are today is the sum of all your past attitude and thoughts. And that means that if you can change your thoughts and attitude today, you can change your future.

You know the old saying, 'is the glass half empty or half full?'

How do you see things, positively or negatively? Do you look for a positive outcome in situations or do you look for a negative outcome?

In the simplest terms, a good attitude is wanting to do the best you can.

How do you feel?

People act on things based on how they feel.

Our emotional side is what makes us do some things and not do others. How you feel about this business is going to have a huge impact on your success.

How you feel about other things is also really important. But - you can learn how to adapt your feelings to help you succeed.

1. How do you feel about the past?

All of us come into this business with our own unique past. Past successes, past failures, past relationships, past disappointments and all of our past experiences.

You can treat your past in two ways.

You can use your past as a stick, to beat yourself over the head with, saying, "If only I had done this," or "if only I had done that, my life would be so much better today". Some people spend their entire lives replaying the past.

The past is not where you want to spend your time.

Here's a better way to treat your past. Use it as a school, a vast resource to learn from and to better yourself with. You got a result from everything you did in the past. It might have been good, or it might have been bad, it doesn't matter; you got a result. From that result you can learn more than you might imagine, to improve your life in the future. Simply study the result and refine your future actions.

Treat your past as a school. You've paid for that education and no one can take it from you! If it's been a harsh education, you can rejoice today, because through that experience, you've become more valuable. It's not the easy times that make you grow.

A good way to look at the past is to take all your years and the knowledge you've gained from them, and invest all of that into this upcoming year.

Today is the first day of your future, not another day of your past. Let today be the day you decide to take your past and use it to create the future you deserve.

2. How do you feel about the future?

The future is an awesome force that you can apply to today's activity.

Why did you join this business? Why are you reading this book?

Not for an immediate result. You're doing it for the future! You can take a well designed future and the inspiration that gives you to find the time and energy to succeed in this business.

I call the future 'the promise'. Now there's a price to pay for that promise, but it's easier to pay when the promise is strong. Plan your future well, and it can become the greatest pull on your life. Any time you are struggling and feeling discouraged, use the promise of your future to help you pay the price you need to today.

On the other hand, if the promise is weak, the price is almost impossible to pay. If you can't see the meaning in your daily activities, if they're not pulling you towards your well planned future, the price can become too much to bear.

So make your future and its pull on you a strong one. It will carry you through almost any adversity.

The key to this is Goal-Setting, which we will look at a little later.

3. How do you feel about other people?

You won't succeed by yourself. We all need other people. We need each other's ideas. We need each other's inspiration. We need each other's strength. We need each other's encouragement. If you think you can succeed without other people, you're mistaken.

But that's not a sign of weakness.

When you understand how valuable other people are is when you become powerful.

4. How do you feel about yourself?

Understanding self-worth is fundamental to your accelerated progress.

I don't know you, but I know something about you; you have greatness within you.

You have the ability to do things that you can't even imagine. You have talents and skills within you that you haven't even begun to reach yet.

It's not important to change how other people view us; what's important is how we view ourselves.

Look at yourself. What could you do? What do you think is your highest potential?

Decide today not to allow other people's negative or mediocre expectations of you become reality. If other people don't expect great things from you, then understand your own self-worth and expect great things from yourself.

Jim Rohn, a man I admire enormously, said:

"The only limitation placed on our abilities is our inability to easily recognise our unlimited nature. It takes effort to become aware of our staggering and limitless abilities. It takes effort to become enthusiastic over a cause; it takes effort to continue when our results, as well as our friends, tell us to give up trying.

It does not, however, take effort to fail. It requires little else than a slowly deteriorating attitude about our present, our future, and ourselves.

It is ironic that one of the few things in this life over which we have total control is our own attitudes, and yet most of us live our entire life behaving as though we had no control whatsoever. By our attitude, we decide to read or not to read. By our attitude, we decide to try or give up. By our attitude, we blame ourselves for our failure or we foolishly blame others. Our attitude determines whether we love or hate, tell the truth or lie, act or procrastinate, advance or recede, and by our own attitude, we, and we alone, actually decide whether to succeed or fail."

The Seven Diseases of Attitude

We need to share some of the things that can hurt you, as well as the things that will help you. It's important to understand the threats we all face, and how to conquer them.

1. Lethargy

Lethargy is the sluggish approach to life. Lethargy is that shrug of the shoulder saying, "I can't be bothered."

I tell you this; if you really can't be bothered, then you won't do it.

So get bothered! Get bothered about your future! Get bothered about your life! Strong feelings are what I'm after.

I am often asked, "What type of people do you want in your team?" or "What type of people do you like to be around?" My answer is always, "People with strong feelings.'

I don't even care what they feel strongly about, as long as they feel strongly about it, because strong feelings will always triumph over lethargy.

Feel strongly.

2. Indecision

Indecision is mental paralysis. Indecision can bring you to your knees. Indecision is when a person says, "I know I'm on the fence but I don't know what to do."

Indecision is the thief of opportunity, time and happiness.

You have to make decisions. It makes no difference what side they're on. What makes a difference is learning the habit of making decisions. A life full of adventure, a life full of success, is a life full of many decisions.

Make the decision and move on.

Learn to decide.

3. Doubt

The worst doubt that a person can have in their life is self-doubt. To have no confidence in themselves.

If you doubt for a period of time, pretty soon you'll get good at doubting. A person can become a practised doubter, and I'll tell you what happens then. You end up with an empty cup, or empty pockets.

The only healthy doubt is the one that is really wanting an answer.

Remember this. Trust is better than doubt. Belief is better than questioning.

I'm not saying that you're going to win with that formula every time, but you'll win with it a lot more than you'll win with doubt. And you'll be happier in the process.

Choose belief over doubt.

4. Worry

Worry can cause you problems; health problems, social problems, personal problems, economic problems.

Remember this. The heavy chains of worry are forged in idle hours.

Repeat. The heavy chains of worry are forged in *idle hours*.

So get busy, and remember that most of what you worry about never happens.

Don't worry.

5. Being over cautious

This is the timid approach to life. Some people are always waiting for better days to come.

But better days won't just turn up. You have to take the days as they are and make them into what you want them to be.

There has never been a better day than today.

One of the biggest fears people have is What if; "What if this happens? What if that happens?" People who fail will always focus on the risk within the opportunity.

People who succeed look at the opportunity within the risk. You can't get away from risk. Nobody goes through life without risk.

Do you think you can have success and happiness without risk? Impossible! Risk is part of our lives. Understand that, accept it, and don't be afraid.

Accept risk.

6. Pessimism

The pessimist always looks on the dark side. The pessimist always looks at why this business won't work. The pessimist doesn't look for virtue. They look for faults and if they find a fault they start to enjoy it.

Pessimists see themselves as smarter than the rest, but they lose the good in life as a result.

The good in life is there for the optimists among us to enjoy.

Be optimistic.

7. Whinging and moaning

Whinging and moaning will get you nowhere. People who whinge and moan are much better served by taking the energy they use to whinge and moan and applying it to constructive or positive action. This would actually get them some results!

If you spend your time complaining, you're wasting time you could be using for much better things.

Don't complain.

The Importance of Goals

A good attitude alone will not make you a success.

If you're driving somewhere and you have the wrong map, or your sat nav has the wrong information in it, a good attitude will just help you get lost with a smile on your face!

A good attitude alone is not enough. You must also have a clear picture of where you're headed. Your plan must consist of clear, specific goals that will help you reach your ultimate goal.

Imagine that your ultimate goal is a holiday in Monte Carlo. Your plan is to drive from where you are to Monte Carlo. Your specific goals are to drive 200 miles a day and in your head is a picture of every stop you will make between here and Monte Carlo.

That's goal-setting.

Try this goal-setting exercise. Try it now:

Write down a clear goal and four good reasons why you believe you will achieve it.

My clear specific goal is:

....

The reasons why I will achieve my clear specific goal are:

1..

2..

3..

4..

List the obstacles you need to overcome to accomplish these goals.

....

....

List the solutions to these obstacles; include the people who can help you.

....

....

List the action steps you need to take each day to achieve your goals, and the date you wish to accomplish them by.

Steps: ....

....

....

....

The date I will achieve this goal is.......................................

Your signature...

Now, just like the holiday in Monte Carlo, you know where you want to go, and you have the map to tell you how to get there.

Your attitude will help drive you to your personal goals.

Your attitude will help you reap the benefits of achieving your goals.

Your attitude will help you overcome every obstacle and challenge that stands between you and your goals.

Your attitude will help you to take action when it would be easier not to.

And always remember: your attitude today is the foundation of your future.

Belief

Belief is the guiding compass that leads us toward our goals and gives us the certainty to know we will get there.

Without belief, or the ability to tap into it, people can be totally defeated. With powerful guiding belief, you can see what you want and you are motivated to get it.

You'll know the saying, 'I'll believe it when I see it.' I say that you must believe it *before* you can see it. That goes for any endeavour in life.

The more I learn about human behaviour, the more I learn about the extraordinary power that belief has over our lives.

A classic example of the power of belief is the four-minute mile.

Before 1954, the consensus was that it was impossible to run a mile in under four minutes. Many scientists and doctors said it was physically impossible. The athletic world proclaimed that it could not be done.

But one man believed he could do it.

On 6 May 1954, Dr. Roger Bannister ran a mile in 3 minutes, 59.4 seconds.

Aside from being an incredible achievement, what is really interesting about this is that within a couple of weeks, six other athletes also ran a mile in under a minute. Within a month, eight others had achieved the same.

How did this happen?

Simply because the athletes who followed Bannister stopped believing that it was impossible and started believing it was possible. History is littered with examples of achievements stemming from great belief; from aviation and space travel, to medical advances and ground-breaking technology.

The moment you start believing your goals, ambitions and dreams are possible, they become possible.

Belief is powerful. If you believe you can or can't do something... you're right.

Your desire and belief system

Your desire is the runway from which you take off for your goals and ambitions.

Your belief is the compass that keeps you on course.

Self-limiting beliefs

You may have a desire to be more successful, to make more money, or to have better personal relationships, but the reality is that without a well formed desire and belief system, self-limiting beliefs will make you crash.

You cannot ignore your self-limiting beliefs. They have been with you a long time, since childhood in many cases. Self-limiting beliefs lead to a negative self-image, a self-image that you did not create.

An example of a self-limiting belief:

Suppose you were asked to walk across a plank of wood, 40 feet long, 3 feet wide and 1 foot thick. It is lying on the ground and you are asked to walk from one end to the other without falling off.

Could you do that? Of course you could.

However, now, the same plank of wood is being used as a bridge between two very high buildings. Could you now walk along the plank? In reality, probably not.

But ask yourself this: has the plank changed in any way?

Obviously, the answer is no.

So what would stop you? The answer is, lack of belief and too much imagination. You imagine, for example; it's too high, I'll slip off, I might get hurt, I'll die!

You imagine all sorts of self-limiting beliefs.

But just as lack of belief and imagination built up your self-limiting beliefs, then belief and imagination can be used to bring them down. And you need to! As you well know, your-self limiting beliefs are real enough, and they will prevent you from achieving your goals.

Fixed beliefs

As well as self-limiting beliefs, we also have fixed beliefs.

Fixed beliefs are primarily the result of our personal history, background and life experience. As both self-limiting beliefs and fixed beliefs are initially formed in childhood, it is important to look at our early years in order to understand them.

Most children learn in two main ways:

1. By imitation.

2. By moving from an uncomfortable experience towards a comfortable experience.

Our very early awareness is that we are helpless and need those closest to us – probably our parents – to give us assistance, love, affection and protection.

We learn to gain the attention of others by moving, and making noises. When we're hungry, we cry until we're fed. When we want affection, we cry until somebody comes and picks us up.

While these actions usually achieve the result we want, they also reinforce the fact that we are dependent.

All of this happened to you. Over the next few years, like most children, you probably dribbled, had trouble with your bowel functions, ate chaotically, etc. All of this was witnessed by many people, whose reactions confirmed to you that as well as being dependent, you were now also grubby, with sticky hands and socially unacceptable.

By the age of four you had probably, to a large degree, developed speech, some mastery of a knife and fork, learned to run and, in general, made great progress.

Far from receiving consistent and generous praise from all of those closest to you, they presented you with the next ordeal in your life... school!

So there you were, merrily trotting off to school. This was the new start.

So what happened?

The older children were smarter, more co-ordinated, better educated and less helpless and, possibly worst of all, they were bigger. You know that's true because they told you so.

So another film of negative self-image formed. This pattern continued throughout your youth and teenage years, until the day you finally left home to 'make your own way'.

The only problem was that as you grew up and got bigger and older, your negative self-image tagged along with you like a shadow...

Our negative self-image has a few key weapons, including the fear of failure and the fear of rejection. These are formed by our exposure to criticism at an early age, which leads us to develop negative habits.

How real is this fear? Very real! And it has been with you a long time.

But you can look at fear in another way:

- **F**alse
- **E**vidence
- **A**ppearing
- **R**eal

According to experts, we are born with just two fears: the fear of loud noises and the fear of falling. That's why children at a very tender age can put their hand in an open flame!

All our other fears we have picked up and brought with us through life.

Now, there are good fears in life and there are destructive fears.

The good fears are about self-preservation; fear of falling, fear of a loud noise or explosion, fear of drowning, fear of fire. These are good fears.

But we also have self-limiting fears; fear of what others think of us, fear of rejection, fear of the unknown, fear of failure, fear of success. These are destructive fears.

What to do about fear? Meet it head on.

Can fear be avoided? The problem with avoiding fear is that it gives credibility to the fear, and will also increase the habitual nature of it.

For example; many people, conditioned from an early age, are afraid of the dark. So they try to avoid the dark, and they sleep with the light on. This gives them temporary relief, but does not address the fear itself, and so it gradually leads to greater fear.

A genuine antidote to fear is action.

Identify your fears and take action to stop them.

If you are fearful of walking under ladders, you walk around them. Take action, and stop walking round ladders!

If you avoid picking up the phone to make an appointment, that is the very action you must do to overcome your fear of the telephone. Pick up the phone, make the call. Make the appointment.

In just a short few calls you will become better at it.

Ralph Waldo Emerson said, "Do what you fear most and the death of fear is certain."

You will either face the fear of doing the business or you will face the fear of not doing the business!

Attack the fear habit. Don't avoid your fears, confront them.

To be successful, you will need belief.

- belief in yourself
- belief in the Company and what it does
- belief in this great industry, Network Marketing.

Positive thinking

Positive thinking, what I call 'realistic optimism', actually works!

The world in your mind is just as real as your external world. Negative thinking prevents you from being in control of your life, while positive thinking puts you in control. Control starts with thoughts, thoughts determine your feelings, and feelings determine your actions, as I discussed earlier.

The law of cause and effect says that every effect has a specific cause. Thoughts are causes.

You will destroy yourself if you continually have negative thoughts.

Think positively, and you will be unstoppable.

I have learned that most people believe that they can think whatever they wish, without consequences. It is not true. Whatever you consistently think about can eventually come true, whether it is positive or negative.

Always think positively.

Your goals

Your goals are a fundamental part of self-development, and of building a successful business. They are what will motivate you, and keep you motivated.

As we have seen, effective goal-setting is made up of two key elements:

1. Having a clear specific goal.

2. Identifying the actions that can help you achieve the goal.

Your goals, combined with an understanding of, and belief in, the actions that will get you there, are your motivation.

We will look at motivation in more detail later.

Personal inventory

This is a short list of assets you need to help achieve your goals. Rate yourself on a scale of one to ten (where ten is strongest) in each of the areas.

Once you determine your strengths and weaknesses, use the list of suggested reading and listening at the end of this book to improve areas where you face an obstacle.

- burning desire
- phone skills
- are you teachable
- drive/determination
- persistence
- confidence
- self reliance
- leadership skills
- commitment.

Excuses

I have heard all the excuses.

Whenever people quit the Utility Warehouse (and they do), they call or email me, and they say, "Steph, I'm quitting today and I want to tell you whose fault it is."

The email may complain that the individual's sponsor didn't train or work with them properly, or the starter pack didn't arrive on time, or the plan didn't work the way it was supposed to... believe me, I have heard them all.

So if in the future you are thinking that you might quit and you're struggling to come up with a reason, just call me and I'll give you an excuse to put in your email. How about: I'm too old, I'm too young, I'm not educated enough, I'm too educated, I don't have the time, nothing any good ever happens to me, I'm not smart enough, I don't have the right background.

I just wish people could be totally honest with me and send me an email that says, "Stephan, I'm quitting today because **that's what I do**. I've done it before and I'll do it again."

Dismantling the excuses

Let's have a quick look at three of the most common excuses I hear, and my answers to them:

Excuse: 'I am too old.' Hogwash! Colonel Sanders was 66 when he started Kentucky Fried Chicken.

Excuse: 'I'm not smart enough.' Baloney! The great majority of the world's most successful people left school with very little formal academic education. It's about attitude, not exam results.

Excuse: 'I just don't have the time.' Rubbish! There are 168 hours in a week. Take off 9 hours a night for sleep, that leaves 105 hours a week. Subtract 10 hours a day for work (and let's assume you work 6 days a week and not 5), that's 60 hours, that leaves 45 hours of spare time. You could fit another working week in that time, and many people do!

For most people, it's not lack of time, it's lack of direction.

Here is a good, positive exercise for you:

Write a list of your strong points, eg. drive, desire, enthusiasm, ambition, attitudes, your skills, whether you are teachable, open-minded, prepared to learn, and so on.

1...

2...

3...

4...

5...

6...

7...

8...

9...

10...

As you can see, you do have strengths. Most of your self-limiting beliefs are, guess what, nonsense!

Many people who are successful and achieve outstanding results only have a few major strengths, but they learn how to make the most of them.

Look again at the strengths that you have.

The entire Impact System™ is about getting favourable results in your life. Those favourable results come from strengths that are deep inside you. That is where they come from and they have always been there.

Look positively at your results and don't beat yourself up. Remember; 'practice makes progress', not perfect.

Think positively, and each time you take an action step in a directed way, you become better.

Association

Never underestimate the power of influence.

Your behaviour will be mostly influenced by ideas. Ideas are mostly influenced by education and education is mostly influenced by the people we associate with.

Influence is powerful and influence is subtle. Influence is powerful because it's so subtle.

The influence of those you spend time with is going to have a profound effect on your success or failure. You've heard the phrase, 'peer pressure'. Peer pressure is simply the people that you associate with, applying their influence to move you toward their way of thinking.

Here's what happens. If you associate with people who spend more than they make, the chances are excellent that you will spend more than you make. If you associate with people who go to the pub five nights a week, the chances are excellent that you'll be there too. If you hang around people who don't read many books, the chances are excellent that you won't either. If the people around you are negative and pessimistic, the chances are excellent that you'll become negative and pessimistic too.

We're not usually going to let someone yank us off course and wreck our lives completely, but we do let them nudge us off course. We let them suggest us off course. We let them bump us off course a little at a time, until finally, ten years later, we find ourselves asking, "How did I get here?"

It's not weakness if this happens. But it is weakness to know it's happening and not do anything about it.

There are three, all-important, questions you need to ask yourself. And you need to tell the truth. Let the days of kidding yourself be over. Don't think that it doesn't matter if you kid yourself. Everything matters.

So be honest.

Questions to ask yourself:

1. Who do I associate with?

2. What are they doing to me?

>   What do they have me listening to?
>
>   What do they have me reading?
>
>   What do they have me thinking?
>
>   How do they have me feeling?
>
>   What do they have me saying?
>
>   What do they have me settling for?

And most importantly: What do they have me becoming?

3. IS THAT OK?

Of course, I don't know your answers to these questions, but you need to ask them and you need to answer them truthfully.

After studying some of the most successful people in the world, Napoleon Hill said, in his book *Think and Grow Rich*, that the number one reason people fail in life is because they listen to their friends, family and neighbours.

Based on your own answers to the three questions above, here are some actions you can take to correct or improve your association.

1. Disassociation

This is the one that shouldn't be taken lightly, but sometimes you need to consider it. Some people keep associating with people they know are bad for them because they don't want to hurt their feelings.

The sad thing about that is, they are literally sacrificing their life because they are afraid of conflict.

Disassociation doesn't need to mean confrontation. Sometimes you can simply ease yourself out of the wrong person's life.

Just be sure when you do this that it's a conscious effort on your part, or you may end up not accomplishing it.

Disassociation is not an easy action to take, but sometimes it's the most important one.

2. Limited association.

You may not want to disassociate completely with some of the people in your life, but it's important that you evaluate how much time you spend with them.

As Jim Rohn suggests, "It's OK to have casual friends, as long as you give them casual time, not serious time. It's OK to spend two hours with some people, but not two days. It's OK to spend two minutes with some people, but not two hours."

Here's how to have an average, mediocre life: spend most of your time on minor things.

Here's how to have a successful life: spend major time with positive influence and minor time with negative influence.

I am not saying that you shouldn't care or have compassion for people you feel are not good for you. You might even be a positive influence in their lives.

I'm just saying that you have to be very careful of the incredible power of influence. Don't be naïve and think it won't have an effect on you.

You must decide what matters to you the most.

3. Good association

Here's the most positive of the three!

Good association means spending more time with the right people; men and women of substance. People who understand philosophy and discipline. People of accomplishment and character.

Ask yourself, "Who could I get close to and spend some time with, that will help me progress?"

I have a phrase that describes the people I spend time with; people who 'think right'.

But if you can't find someone right away, you can always start with CDs, books or seminars to give you some daily positive influence, and then you'll start attracting some people who 'think right' too.

But that's one of the greatest aspects of our business; how easy it is to associate with the right people. And this is what the Company training is all about. Until you start to attract the right people, we'll try to give you as much positive influence as we possibly can.

This is called 'association on purpose'. Picking out situations and people where you know associating with them will help you to progress.

New Distributors (and the not-so-new as well!)

Although it is always incredibly important, association has the greatest effect on your business when you're first starting out. You need to be very aware of the effect the people around you are having on your business in the early stages.

While you're starting out, it's best to limit your association with people who don't share your feelings about your ability, and your feelings about this business.

You don't need people to discourage you right now – you need encouragement and support.

And there are a lot of negative opinions about Network Marketing out there – you've got better things to do than listen to them.

More than anything else, try to expand your positive associations as much as possible.

That's why the Career Opportunity Presentations (or 'COPs') that the Company arranges, College of Excellence training and events are so important. Attend as many as you can.

And start feeding your mind by reading books and listening to CDs. By reading 15 pages of a good book a day and listening to a training CD a day, you will increase your knowledge and increase your chances of success.

To summarise: Don't join an easy crowd.

Most of the time, we rise only to the expectations of those around us. If those expectations are low, that's probably as far as you will stretch.

Make sure your expectations are high!

Leadership

Leaders are solutions-oriented people. Leaders are unselfish givers, not takers.

Negative complainers never achieve great results; they **damage the belief** of people around them and are no fun to work with.

Problem-solving is one of the number one skills that a true leader should possess. You can look through history and identify the greatness of the leader by the scale of the problems they were able to solve. I have had the good fortune to be around some seriously successful people. The thing they do differently from other people is solve bigger problems. It seems the bigger the problem they solve, the bigger the income they earn.

Simple formula:

> Problem solving = Maturity
>
> Maturity = Personal Growth
>
> Personal Growth = Production.

And I have found:

> Problem Solving = Income.

So when faced with a problem, don't bury your head in the sand and hope the problem goes away; see how many problems you can solve. If you do that, you will become a better problem-solver. Being a poor problem-solver will result in you being a poor income earner.

Think about babies, and how they deal with problems. They can be hungry, tired and sleepy; they might need to be changed or they might have wind. If a baby has one of those problems, how do they try to rectify it? They cry and whinge. That's how they try to solve their problems, because that's all they know how to do.

Now think about adults, and how they deal with problems. If they are a poor problem-solver, what do they do? Yes, you've guessed it, they cry and whinge! They don't try to solve the problem; they try to lay blame on someone else. But adults should know better.

If you cry and whinge, understand that for your income to go up massively, your problem-solving ability has to be cultivated and improve.

Become a good problem-solver. Become a person people can turn to in times of crisis. Remember that most problems you will be dealing with have little to do with rules or regulations; they are mostly personality problems, people crying and whinging and laying the blame on someone else.

How to solve your own problems

The problems that are the most difficult to solve are the ones where you are personally, emotionally, involved. When you are emotionally involved it is tricky to make the right decision.

Ask yourself these questions:

1. **What can I do?** Honestly evaluate your options; some solutions require eating a little humble pie. If that is the right step, be mature enough to admit that, and do it.

2. **What can I read?** I can guarantee that no matter what problem you are facing, someone has written about how to solve it.

3. **Who can I ask?** If you have done all you can and you have read all you can read, then the third step is: 'Who can I ask?' If you ask first, you will never become a skilled problem-solver, you will always be dependent on someone else.

How to solve other people's problems

Three questions to ask:

1. **What can you do about yesterday?** The obvious answer is: nothing.

2. **Are you there to be part of the problem or part of the solution?** That should determine your attitude towards them solving it. Their answer should be, 'To be part of the solution.'

3. **Do you understand there is no perfect solution to anything?** Hopefully, they will agree.

When you've asked those three questions, proceed with dealing with the problem:

1. **Gather the facts.** You will know when you have gathered enough facts, when the picture starts to repeat itself from both sides. There are two sides to every story.

2. **Understand spotlighting.** That is when someone does not want you to notice their faults, so they quickly put the spotlight on the other person to expose theirs. In a personality situation, here is a good rule of thumb; whoever raises the problem first is usually the person at fault and most situations are personality-related.

3. Brainstorm for possible solutions. Ask yourself, "Would this solution work the same every time in the same circumstances?" If it wouldn't, you are probably emotionally involved and you should ask someone else's opinion.

4. Model yourself on someone you respect as a good problem-solver/leader. Ask yourself: "How would they handle this?"

5. Choose the best solution quickly, act upon the solution you choose, make your decision and don't look back. Understand that you are not going to make the correct decision every time. If you make what turns out to be a poor decision, learn from it so you can make a better one next time. Move on.

None of us can avoid the storms of life. To be a Leader, and to be in for the long run will require you, from time to time, to stand against the opinions of the crowd. You may have to swim against the current and stand up for what you believe in.

You will need to work harder and smarter.

You will need to invest your time into those things that will help you build a strong and secure future. You will have set-backs, but you will be strong enough to get up again. You will have learnt from your mistakes and will have improved your business based on action, experience and acquired wisdom.

You can do all of this.

Motivation

If you're going to make this work, if you want this business to give you the opportunity to make big changes in your life, if you want to keep going when times get tough (because they will), then focus on these five key elements that will fire your motivation:

1. Desire

You have to want it. You have to develop your desire. Desire comes from deep within you, but desire can be cultivated. It can be cultivated through the Impact System™. It can be cultivated by getting involved with the right group of people. It can be cultivated by having clear goals. It can be cultivated in many ways.

Cultivate your desire.

2. Decision

You have to know what you want. Many people I meet can tell me what they don't want. Most people spend more time planning their two-week holiday every year than they do planning their future.

Decide what you want.

3. Action

Decision turns you in a new direction; action takes you towards that new direction. Here is a great word that goes with action: massive. Take massive action. Don't be like the

Distributor who says, "I will just hand out a few brochures and see how it goes." They will always be broke. Don't be like the one who says, "I will try a home meeting and see what happens." You can guess their bank account. If you are going to take action, make sure it is all-out massive action. That is where real success comes from.

Take massive action.

4. Feeling sick and tired

Sick and tired means you don't like your life as it is. You have had it up to here. You're not putting up with it any more. It's the point where you say to yourself, "I am sick and tired of being sick and tired. I want change!"

You can live your life one way for years and years. But then one day you draw a line in the sand. You say "I'm sick and tired of this." That can be the day your life changes forever.

Don't put up with sick and tired.

5. Tenacity

Tenacity means, "I will do whatever it takes." Tenacity means, "You can count on me. I will be there."

You pick your mountain in life and wherever that mountain is, you say, "I am going to the top." There will be some people who will tell you, "You can't climb mountains, you don't have the experience." You say, "I am going to the top." Somebody else may say, "Choose another mountain, that one's too steep and rocky." You say, "I am going to the top." Someone else may say, "Come on, not that one. That's too slippery. Climb this other, easier one." You say, "I'm going to the top."

Somebody else may simply say it can't be done. You say, "Listen, I am going to the top. You're either going to see me waving from the top or collapsed on the side—I'm not coming back."

Remember the times in your life when you took a casual approach or had a weak attitude? I bet you didn't accomplish what you set out to accomplish.

When you are climbing your mountain you have got to have a do or die attitude. That's called major tenacity. It is also the difference between success and failure.

There is something about a stubborn, do or die attitude; it works. Nothing can stand in your way.

Have a do or die attitude.

Producing fruit

"If a tree is given minimal nourishment, it will survive but have slow growth. If nourishment is given over what is needed for life, the tree will grow in all directions; but if a tree is given nourishment over and beyond what is needed to support life, needed for growth and more, it will produce fruit - fruit is the overflow, surplus of excess nourishment."

John Grapey

We, as individuals, are like this. And in Network Marketing, our businesses are a reflection of us; if you want your business to grow and bear fruit, you must grow and bear fruit yourself.

And what is your nourishment?

Books and CDs

If you do not read, you must change. Start reading.

If you do not listen, you must change. Start listening.

Start learning.

For your life to change, the change must start with you.

You're reading this book. That's a good start!

PART 2

GETTING
STARTED RIGHT

Building a team – leveraging time

Building a team is the basic principle of Network Marketing, what it's all about.

It's how you create a big business, from small amounts of regular work of your own.

	Team members at start of month	Each team member introduces one person	You introduce one person	Total team members at end of month
Jan	-	-	1	1
Feb	1	+ 1	+ 1	= 3
Mar	3	+ 3	+ 1	= 7
Apr	7	+ 7	+ 1	= 15
May	15	+ 15	+ 1	= 31
June	31	+ 31	+ 1	= 63
July	63	+ 63	+ 1	= 127
August	127	+ 127	+ 1	= 255
Sept	255	+ 255	+ 1	= 511
Oct	511	+ 511	+ 1	= 1,023
Nov	1,023	+ 1,023	+ 1	= 2,047
Dec	2,047	+ 2,047	+ 1	= 4,095

Look at what happens if you introduce just one person a month, and teach all of those individuals to do the same. Just imagine what will happen when each get a few customers!

So, by introducing – or sponsoring – just 12 people and teaching them to do the same, your group has grown to over 4,000 in just one year!

It doesn't always work like this, of course. But if your team grows to only a quarter of the amount in this example, 25% of 4,095 is still a group of around 1,000 people.

John Paul Getty said: "I would much rather have 1% of a hundred people's efforts, than 100% of my own." Wise words!

1,000 people x 1 hour worked each = 1,000 hours per week. That's a good business.

So let's see how you do it.

First steps for the new Distributor

1. Become your own first customer

The Impact System^{TM} assumes that you have signed up for all the basic services that the Utility Warehouse provides.

If you want to earn a substantial residual income in this business, please don't be naive and think you don't need to use the services yourself.

You can't be a Mercedes dealer and turn up to work in a BMW! It wouldn't instil confidence and belief in the customers.

But there's more to it. It's very important you obtain all the services that the Company provides for your own use, for many reasons:

- **For your personal benefit.** You'll save money!

- **Develops knowledge.** You'll understand how the products and services work.

- **Increases belief in the services.** You'll understand how good the Company is at what it does.

- **As you use all of the services, you will develop the belief and conviction necessary to share them effectively.** People buy because of how you feel about the benefits of the services, not because of how much you know about them.

So, sign up for the services. You'll also find that your best sales tool will be your Utility Warehouse bill.

2. Make time

The next step is to make a specific time commitment to building your business. Then use that time for productive activity.

The Impact System^{TM} is designed to support long-term, sustained commitment.

This is not a lottery. It's not a game of chance. To build a successful business takes time and effort.

Consistency and persistence will be the biggest determining factors in your long-term success.

3. Start to educate yourself

First off:
- Watch the *What's it all about?* DVD.
- Watch it again.
- Listen to *Building your Network Marketing Business* by Jim Rohn.

Read, listen to and watch everything you can get your hands on that will positively impact the way you function in this business.

Read the Company Compensation Plan and highlight it; you can avoid all kinds of future mistakes if you understand the rules at the start.

Become fully informed about how our business works.

4. Lead by example

Your future team will do what you did when you got started. Start leading by example now.

Set up a time within 48 hours to meet with your sponsor/upline.

Do not take this meeting lightly! I believe it is imperative that you meet with your sponsor/upline in the first 48 hours, either face to face, over the phone or in a group setting. This meeting is what I call, 'The Game Plan Overview'. The Company calls this Meeting 1, and provides you with forms to help you do the meeting.

This is how the meeting works. Remember, it's for you this time, but it's for your team members in future.

The Game Plan Overview (Meeting 1).

a. Make sure you're using the services.

b. Make your time commitment. Commit to a specific amount of time you will give exclusively to your new business. This needs to include time for phone calls, presentations, meetings and trainings.

The number of hours per day I will commit: _____

The number of days per week I will commit: _____

Will I commit to at least one year? _____

c. Start on your contact list – this shows the size of your immediate market.

d. Development plan for the next 30 days after your training. This little sheet will help you stay on track and achieve your goals.

e. The compensation plan. Go over the compensation plan with your sponsor/upline to understand how to attain and qualify for additional bonuses.

f. Your goals and ambitions.

g. Target dates to achieve the following positions:

- Qualified Distributor_____
- Team Leader_____

5. Listen to *Making the Shift* by Darren Hardy during your second day

6. Complete your list. You will have spoken about this when you met your sponsor/upline. Take the time in the first few days to complete your contact list.

7. Listen to *Making the Shift* during your third day.

8. Start your training. Log on to the Extranet and do the online training. Do it again. Do it as much as you need to make sure you understand what the Company does.

9. Get three-way calling. Three-way calling is a very effective tool, especially if you want your sponsor/upline's help in recruiting a group. It's a minimal cost, and well worth it. Call Customer Service to get it.

10. Get a diary, and use it. It's so important to make sure you schedule a Career Opportunity Presentation (COP) every fortnight.

11. Get a diary, and use it. It's so important to make sure you schedule your College of Excellence Training.

12. Get a diary, and use it. It's so important to make sure you schedule upcoming special events.

13. Identify your upline. If you don't know who they are – call Partner Services and find out!

14. Get your questions answered. Be sure to have any concerns or questions answered at this time. Ask your upline, or Partner Services.

15. Keep a tight rein on your new team members! They may be full of enthusiasm, but tell them not to say anything to anyone about the services or the opportunity until you have gone through some basic scripts with them. If they go off before they're ready, they will not succeed, which means they will get disheartened, and they will stop.

16. Make sure all your new team members have an answer service. You're going to want to be able to leave them messages!

17. Make sure your new team members do numbers 1 –16.

Prepare to take action

When you take action, the first thing you need to do is think.

I take great comfort in thinking about those who have gone before and built a large team. They've mastered the '10-ton telephone' (it feels that hard to pick up!) and they've become successful.

I suppose that's why we all need mentors. We all need to have somebody putting positive input into our life, even if it is just to give us a push along.

My goal is to get you to pick up the phone and make the call. If I can help you do that, I have served you well.

I am constantly thinking about how I can creatively communicate truths that have been written about before by many people in Network Marketing. But my aim is simple enough. When I share what I have learned with you, I am trying to open up your mind, so that you can begin to think and take action.

Here are some of the questions I ask myself:

Why is it that two people can sit in the same seminar and hear the same words, yet one will leave that seminar and achieve great success while the other will continue in their mediocrity?

Why is that?

Why is it that someone with little or no formal education can still attain great wealth, while educated people can end up with nothing?

Why is that?

Why is it that people with small talent and great resolve achieve so much, while others with great talent and no resolve achieve so little?

Why is that?

And - what separates a winner from a loser?

Here are a few questions for you to ask yourself:

"What will happen if I don't make that telephone call?"

"What might happen if I do make that telephone call?"

"Where will I be in five years if I do what they have shown me to do?"

"Where will I be in five years if I put my feet up and don't follow the basic instructions in this little book, which is designed to help me get to where I want to be in five years?"

Questions are powerful simply because they encourage you to think. If we don't question ourselves, we simply float down the river like everybody else.

Questioning pushes us out of our comfort zone and into the area where we are required to take action.

Why is that?

Here's a question that has spurred me on:

"What will happen if I take this action, and what will happen if I don't do it?"

It is the kind of question that makes you feel uncomfortable. It causes you to take a serious look at your life. It makes you take stock of where you are, what you're doing and where you're going.

Questions that cause us to think about our life will prepare us to take the next successful step.

They will prepare us to take action.

Contacting and inviting

If you are successful in getting people to look at the business, you will be successful in building a team. The bottom line is that much of your success will result from inviting people in the right way

Who to invite

With a bit of work, you should be able to make a list of over 100 people you know by name.

Give everyone you know and meet the opportunity to see this business and make their own decision. It is not your responsibility to make everyone see this business as you do, or to try and convince people that it's the business for them.

Your only responsibility is to share it with everyone and let them make their own decision.

Don't prejudge someone based on your assumptions – you have no idea really who may or may not want to take up this opportunity. Have an open mind. You may well be surprised.

How to invite

There are lots of ways you can contact and invite people. You may choose to explore different methods as you grow your business. But to start with, focus on contacting and inviting people by phone. This way, you will develop vital communication skills that will serve you well at the start of your business, and that you will be able to build on later as well.

The purpose of the 'inviting' phone call is to set up an appointment for your prospect – someone you think will be interested in the business – to look at the business. Your goal should be to create curiosity and excitement. Answer as few questions as possible and get a firm commitment from them to look at the business.

It's important for you to understand one vital point, and make sure your new Distributors understand it too: never try to explain this business over the phone.

We have tools that can help you explain our business opportunity, but they work best when you're face-to-face with someone.

Over the phone, it's really easy to give the wrong impression of what this business is about.

I was approached by several people about Telecom Plus in the early days. Over the phone, they gave me the impression that this was a telephone sales door-knocking job... and guess what, I didn't listen to them!

It's important to get in front of someone to show them the business.

Different approaches

One important point to remember is: you are not the issue!

You are the messenger, not the message. Please do not think you need to be successful first before you share the business opportunity with someone. Your objective is to share the information, and sell them on how good the business is, not on how good you are.

Commit to the process of becoming a good inviter.

Understand that the best you can do today is not the best you will do in the future; it's just the best you can do today.

You will learn something new from every contact you make.

Another key to remember is never to apologise during the invite. You are coming from a point of strength here; our business is not on trial or test.

There are basically three different approaches you can use (and teach!) for contacting prospects:

- the direct approach
- the indirect approach, and
- the 'Who do you know?' approach.

The direct approach

Use this approach with people you know well; people you feel have a good level of respect or friendly feelings toward you.

If you are new to the business, I would suggest the conversation should last no more than a few minutes and you should always start the call with, "It's just a quick call because I am running late for," eg. an appointment or picking up the children, so you can get off the phone once you've made the appointment and not get dragged into trying to explain the business over the phone.

Example:

"Hi John. It's Stephan. How are you? [etc] It's just a quick call as I'm on my way out. May I ask you, is the time right for you to look at other ways of making money? Are you open to looking at business opportunities?"

The answer will be "Yes", "No" or "What's it about?"

Tell them you would like to explain it over the phone but it will take too long and besides, you're running late as it is... it will be far easier to show them because you have something they need to see.

Tell them you're free tomorrow or the next day. Does that fit in with them?

Here is another example:

"Hi Mary. It's Stephan. How are you? [etc] It's a quick call as I'm just on my way out... Look, if I could show you a way to set up an additional income stream without interfering with your job or business, could you find thirty minutes in the next couple of days to look at it?"

Here is another example:

This is good for anyone you know who is dissatisfied in any area of their life. It could be that they hate their job/boss, they're afraid of redundancy, would like more holidays, to upgrade the car, pay for something special for a loved one, etc... but they can't afford it.

"Hi John. It's Stephan. How are you? [etc] It's just a quick call because I am on my way out to an appointment at the bank. Can I ask you something? A while ago you said you hated your

job and would like out. Were you serious or joking?" [John says he is serious] *"I can't go into it now but I might have a way out for you. Can we get together for thirty minutes tomorrow or the next day so I can run an idea by you?"*

Or it could just be as simple as:

"Mary, I'm glad I got hold of you! Listen, I only have a minute. I'm just running out of the door, but I have something I need to talk to you about. How soon could we get together?"

Example: approaching existing customers to become distributors

"Hi John/Mary...its just a quick call. I know you have been a customer for a while now, well the UWDC are looking for satisfied customers to become distributors and there is a Business opportunity presentation on Monday evening at the ..... I would appreciate it if you could come along to find out about it and how it could benefit you."

The indirect approach

You should use this approach when you are contacting someone who might be perceived to be better or more successful than you; in other words, when you are 'recruiting up'.

The perception has nothing to do with the reality.

'Recruiting up' does not mean they actually are better than you or me; it simply means they may have a bigger circle of influence or a better contact base than you. The basic philosophy of this approach is to play yourself down, and play up to their ego, their sense of their own importance.

Example:

"Hello Mr. Smith. How are you? It's Stephan Longworth here. It's just a very quick call. I have always had a lot of respect for you in business. I am getting involved in an opportunity that has some really exciting potential and I would really value your professional opinion on it. Could we get together for twenty minutes tomorrow or [another day] so I can run an idea by you?"

Example:

"Hello Mary. It's Stephan Longworth. How are you? It's just a quick call. I've always had a lot of respect for you and the success you have had in business. May I ask you - do you keep your income options open?" ["Yes"] "Great. I can't go into it now, as I am late for an appointment, but can we get together tomorrow or [another day] for 20 minutes? I want to run an idea by you."

The 'Who do you know?' approach

You should use this approach for people who are very successful, or if you don't know if they are 'dissatisfied'.

It's basically, "Who do you know who would like to make more money?"

It gives them the chance to say, "What about me?" if they are interested. Or they may give some names of people they know if the timing is not right for them.

Example:

"John, it's Stephan. Just a quick call. I have joined a very exciting company, listed on the London stock market, and we are looking for some sharp people who might be interested in setting up a lucrative additional income stream without affecting their job/business. Who do you know that would fit that description?"

Example:

"Mary, it's Stephan. Just a quick call, as I am on my way out. You have been on my mind to call. Can I ask you - who do you know that is entrepreneurial and would like to make some serious money part-time? We are expanding in your area."

Example:

If you are talking to someone you've just met, the normal questions come up, "Where are you from?" and, "What do you do?"

Here's how to use this approach.

"Where about are you from?" [They answer] "Really? The company I do business with is looking at expanding in that area! May I ask - who do you know that I could give some information to that would like to make more money?" ["Me!"]

Re-contacting people you have told about the business

There are countless examples of people who have joined our business 12-36 months after they were first approached.

If people on your list do not join, you must re-contact them every three months. Their circumstances might have changed.

Example:

"Mary, hi, it's Stephan. It's just a quick call to touch base with you. Do you remember a while ago I showed you/spoke to you about our business? I must apologise because I didn't do it justice or show you the bigger picture. I have been involved for a while now and it's going really well. Would it be OK if I sent you the latest information, so you can evaluate it properly for yourself? I understand the timing might not be right for you, but you might know someone who would be interested. Thanks."

You have nothing to lose by doing this – and everything to gain, as does your prospect!

Answering questions, overcoming objections

The majority of people that you contact will have some questions or objections. These will usually be out of curiosity, if you have done your job correctly. So with that in mind, it is important to be prepared for the questions and objections that will come up.

Let's look at the most common ones:

1. What they said: "What is it?" or "Tell me more!"

What they meant: "What is it?" or "Tell me more!"

This is only natural. Here are a few responses to that question:

"John, I would if I could but as I said, I am running a bit late. And what I need to share with you is 90% visual."

"Mary, it's like a haircut; you need to be there to fully understand what I'm talking about."

"John, I can appreciate your question and I don't want to sound evasive over the phone. All I can tell you is this is a massive opportunity with a PLC business with lots of high-street names joining. If I could effectively explain it over the phone I would, but I need to show you how it works."

"Mary, if I could, I would, but I am too new in the business to explain it to you effectively over the phone. I need to show you."

And get a commitment...

"That is why we need to get together a.s.a.p. Is tomorrow good for you or would the next day be better?"

2. What they said: "I don't have the time."

What they meant: "You haven't shown me enough value to justify my time."

Responses:

"John, I wouldn't ask you to give up any of your time if I didn't think it would be worth your while."

"I fully understand and appreciate how valuable your time is. But if I could show you a way to create a second revenue stream using my time and your contacts; would you be willing to spend 30 minutes with me to get the facts?"

"Mary, I am only asking for 30 minutes. If I am wrong, you've lost half an hour. But what if I'm right?"

"John, when I thought of who I would like to work with and who could benefit most from this business, I thought of you. If you can't find 30 minutes to check it out that's OK, but I was just thinking of you."

And get a commitment...

"I can work around your diary; would daytime or evening be better for you?"

3. What they said: "Is this Network Marketing?"

What they meant: "Is this Network Marketing?"

Response:

Ask them what they know about Network Marketing.

If the answer is positive, just say, "Great. What do you know about the industry?"

If the answer is negative, point out that the Utility Warehouse is a PLC, listed on the London Stock Exchange. They have taken the best bits from the industry and discarded the worst bits and they're taking Network Marketing into the 21st century.

And get a commitment...

"When can we get together so I can show you the facts on the company?"

4. What they said: "Is it pyramid selling?"

What they meant: "Is it legal and ethical?"

Responses:

"I am not sure what a pyramid is, can you explain it to me?" [They usually can't, but will try to give an answer so they don't look like an idiot] *"This is nothing like that!"* [Point out the credibility and the fact that the Company is a PLC on the London Stock Exchange].

"John, if this was what you think it is, I would not be involved in it. You really need to look at it and get the information before you make any judgment! You're absolutely right, though, it is important for a business to be legal and ethical and after you have looked at the facts, I hope you will see that this is, and that will answer your concerns."

5. What they said: "I need to talk to my partner."

What they meant: "I need reassurance and support. Can you help me?"

Response:

"I think the best thing to do is for all three of us to sit down and discuss it together. That way your partner will get all the information also and then the two of you can make a decision."

And get a commitment...

"Does that make sense? Would you like to get together for lunch tomorrow or would Sunday be better?"

6. What they said: "What is the name of the company?"

What they meant: "What is the name of the company?"

Response:

"It's the Utility Warehouse, which is a major company that is operated by Telecom Plus PLC. Have you heard of Telecom Plus? It's incredible what they have been able to accomplish, even in the recession."

And get a commitment...

"When can we get together so I can show you the information and benefits?"

7. What they said: "I'm not interested!"

If they say this, you have said too much! Say less next time.

Give them a recruitment tool – a CD (*UK's Best Kept Secret*)/DVD (*What's it all About?*) or brochure – and ask them at least to review the information before they make a decision.

The feel/felt/found approach

One of the best tools for overcoming objections is the feel/felt/found approach.

You never want to get into an argument over a question or an objection. You want to help them get past it. This approach helps you do that. Here is how it works:

Prospect: "I don't have the time."

*"Mary, I know exactly how you **FEEL**, I **FELT** the same way, but let me tell you what I **FOUND**. You don't need a lot of time to get started, in fact, I have only put a few hours per week in to help create a financial safety net for the future and it's great."*

Prospect: "I don't have the money."

*"John, I know how you **FEEL**, I **FELT** the same way. I was unsure about finding the money, but this is what I **FOUND**. Once I checked it all out, I felt comfortable with the UWDC because they have a refund policy. I felt comfortable finding the money because there was no risk, for a very big opportunity."*

You get the idea. Try this with any objection; I think you will be pleasantly surprised with the results. You are agreeing with them by saying, "I know how you feel. I felt the same way", and you're giving them the solution by telling them what happened to you.

It is a powerful technique.

Getting a firm commitment

Get a commitment from a prospect as to:

- Location – where to meet
- Time – when to meet
- Date – what day to meet
- Partner – who to meet

And...

- That they will be there!
- That they will do you the courtesy of letting you know if they are unable to make the appointment.

Or get a commitment that they will review any information that you send; CD (*UK's Best Kept Secret*)/DVD (*What's it all About?*), brochure, etc...

- That they will listen or view it within 24 hours and get back to you.

How do you get a commitment?

Your prospect's two greatest motivations are the fear of loss and the desire for gain.

Fear of loss is when people feel they will miss out if they don't do something. Advertisers bombard us with fear of loss everywhere we turn; half-price furniture sale, one day only... beat the price increase till Tuesday; two for one offer while stocks last... limited offers are given with a deadline and the items for sale are restricted to a definite time frame.

I have found that the best way to get people to review your information or come to a COP or home meeting is the threat of a 'take away'.

Example: *"Mary, watch this DVD tonight, it's only 15 minutes long, but I need it back asap because I have Tom waiting to watch it."*

What you must convey is, "I would love to have you on board, but I am going to go on with this, with or without you". It's not an arrogant attitude, it's a point of strength attitude.

No-one wants to be part of your test.

If they think you're just dabbling at this business they won't come to your COP or home meeting.

Don't tell your prospect that there is a COP every fortnight for the next 12 months; if they think they can put it off, they won't attend. You need to inject urgency and fear of loss.

Example: *"John, you said you were interested in our business, what are you doing next Tuesday evening for an hour that can't be put off? We are holding a company overview at the [hotel]. It will give you a clear understanding of the opportunity. I'm not sure when the next one is after that, and I don't want you to miss out."*

The close

Just... get off the phone!

Many new Distributors spend a few minutes making the appointment and because they can't quite believe it happened, they spend the next 10 minutes cancelling it! After you have confirmed their commitment to meet with you, it is important to get off the phone.

Call to confirm

This is so important. Some people are afraid to call their prospect to confirm the appointment, but it is **critical** that you do. I am sure you would prefer to know if they can't make the appointment before you drive across town and waste your valuable time.

When you are calling to confirm the appointment, make sure to start the call by telling your prospect that you're in a hurry, but that they will not be disappointed when you meet. Do not start answering more questions.

Commitment

You won't succeed in presenting this business without commitment. Let's look at what that means:

Belief

It is absolutely imperative that you believe in what you are promoting. If you don't believe the Utility Warehouse can provide a person with a financial back-up plan or a good part-time business, or if you don't believe in the services the Company provides, then you won't – and shouldn't – try to convince someone else to believe in them.

Be a good listener

To get really good, you must be a good listener. People will constantly be communicating their feelings towards your presentation through how they act and what they say.

A good listener listens to understand where the other person is coming from, and does not have a quick reply.

A good listener understands that it's more important to listen to the prospect than it is to show them how much they know about this business.

So listen more, and talk less.

Desire

Without the desire to help someone towards a positive result, you simply will not be successful. You must recognise the importance of 'closing', and have the desire to be able to influence your prospect towards taking a positive action that could well change their life for the better.

Plan

Start with the end in mind.

It is important to know where you are going before you start your presentation. The plan or goal for every presentation is to either sponsor them into the business, get them to try the services or get a referral. Go into the presentation with that in mind.

Learn to persuade

Do not spend all of your time trying to impress your prospect. Spend your time persuading the prospect to take action and your time will be rewarded.

Have courage

You need to speak to people about the benefits of the business opportunity and services. It might be a little uncomfortable at first, but you have to do it if you want to be successful.

Through sheer repetition, you will gain the confidence necessary to become successful.

You need to have the courage to present the opportunity and to help people make a decision, rather than procrastinate.

Learn to handle rejection

Whatever happens, you will get some no's.

No matter how fantastic your presentation, no matter if you have done everything right, you will still get them (there's a good CD and book about this - *Go for No*). The no's come with the territory and you need to learn how to handle rejection when it occurs.

First, regard every rejection as an opportunity to learn. Review your presentation and approach. You can even ask your prospect if there was anything you might have said or done to make it better; how you could improve next time?

Second, remind yourself that in this business, as in many other businesses, it's a numbers game. You must understand that a certain percentage of people you contact are going to say no.

You can't hope to be perfect every time, but you can improve your effectiveness by improving your presentation. Just keep stepping up to the spot to take the shot and eventually you will hit the goal.

- Colonel Sanders of Kentucky Fried Chicken fame made close to 1,000 calls and spent nights sleeping in his car before he made his first sale.

- Thomas Edison failed many times before he succeeded in changing our world by creating the incandescent light bulb.

- Andrew Lindsay MBE, our Chief Executive, lost plenty of boat races before he won his Olympic Gold medal.

Finally, do not take the no's as a personal rejection. Don't get upset; sometimes you win, sometimes you lose. That's just the way it is.

Different ways to present the business opportunity

There are several different ways to present the benefits of the business opportunity effectively, but whichever method you are using, they all have this in common:

Elements of the presentation:

- Company
- Services
- Support
- Compensation

Goal for each presentation:

- Involve the prospect in the opportunity
- Create a Club member
- Get referrals

Different methods of presenting the business

1. One-on-one

This method should be one of your most successful ways of presenting the opportunity. One of the biggest positives is the fact that most people are happy to meet you in a one-on-one setting, and the more people see the business, you will be more successful!

How to conduct a one-on-one presentation

- Invite your prospect! Go through the procedure described before, in *Contacting and inviting*

- Dress for business

- Have your own bill with you

- Take your presentation folder; an information pack including brochure/DVD/CD

- Be punctual

- Ask questions and show interest in them. Your aim is to find out what is important to your prospects and then use it later in your presentation

- Tell your story. In a brief way, share how you got involved and why you're excited about it

- Share the elements of the business: the Company, credibility, services

- Show them the money: do the Martini presentation

- Discuss, 'What's in it for them?' No one will join just to help you with your dreams and goals

- When you asked your prospect some questions at the beginning of the presentation, you should have gathered some clues as to what was your prospect's 'hot button'; what it is they really want. Show them how they can achieve what they desire by becoming a Utility Warehouse Distributor

- Move towards a positive result; either signing as a Distributor or agreeing to a second exposure at a local

COP. Your prospect should then have had enough information to make an informed decision.

The Career Opportunity Presentation (COP), Hotel or Home meetings

- Invite your prospects!
- Invite three times the number of people you would like to attend
- Call to confirm
- Dress for business
- On your way to the COP, pick up your top prospect
- Be prepared; take application forms! Also, have some information available (recruiting CDs and DVDs). If they don't sign up there and then, don't let your prospects go home empty-handed.

Home or hotel meetings

These are probably one of the fastest ways to build your team because you can expose many people at a time to the business opportunity.

Have some pleasant music playing. For home meetings, have some snacks and drinks available. Make sure the room is cool; you don't want the room to be overheated and uncomfortable. Set up enough chairs for about two-thirds of the number of people you expect. Add chairs as more people arrive, if you need to.

Please note: don't invite people with a history of a negative attitude to these presentations.

- Welcome your guests. Avoid talking about the business before the meeting. Ask people about their favourite subject; themselves! If they ask how many people you are expecting, say, "A few". That way they won't know if you have had a low or high turnout

- Never leave the room while the meeting is in progress

- Ask people to turn their phones to silent and hold questions until the end

- Tell your story. In a brief way, share how you got involved and why you're excited about it

- Share the elements of the business: the Company, credibility, services

- Show them the money; do the Martini presentation

- Ask your prospects, "Would you like to give it a go?" Moving towards a positive decision at the end of the presentation, the close is the most important part of the process. If you don't ask, "Would you like to give it a go?" it does not matter how well you conducted your meeting.

If they say yes, arrange a get-together in the next 48 hours.

If they say no, thank them and ask, "Who do you know that might benefit from this?"

In either case, make sure they do not go home empty-handed!

The internet and your hosted web site

These are a quick way to get a prospect to review the business, which you can use face-to-face or at a distance.

It is effective for a few reasons:

- It is a very non-threatening approach for your prospect
- It is more time effective
- You are not the issue
- They can see the support that's available.

Explain how the money works (do the Martini presentation) and how this can benefit them.

DVD and Audio Presentation

The CD (*UK's Best Kept Secret*) and DVD (*What's it all About?*) presentations are a great way to share the business with busy people, professionals, cold prospects, etc.

They work well because people do not need to take lots of time out of their lives to hear about the business. The audio is powerful because they can listen to it when they're driving (and there is no more dead time than driving time!).

Many sceptical people are totally turned around after reviewing the DVD or listening to the CD. If it interests them, they can listen to it or watch it over and over again.

The CD and DVD are also excellent tools for a prospect's second exposure to the business, if they've already been to a home meeting, one-on-one, or COP.

The DVD/CD can be an incredibly effective use of your time. Give them out and you can have loads of presentations happening and working for you simultaneously!

They are also a great way to show the business long-distance.

The follow-up

This is where you make money.

Most of the time, what separates the 'I will be,' from the 'I want to be,' can be directly attributed to their willingness and ability to follow up – consistently.

Once you have worked your way through your contact list, you will be left with six scenarios:

1. People you tried, but couldn't get in touch with.

Put these people on a daily follow-up list and discipline yourself to make just three follow-up calls a day. This will take no more than a few minutes in the nooks and crannies of the day. There is no excuse that you haven't got time!

Or send them a 'priority' package with a CD (*UK's Best Kept Secret*) or DVD (*What's it all About?*), *The Independence* newspaper and a brief note asking them to please review the information and call you back a.s.a.p.

2. People you contact, and invite to meet and who say no.

If the person refuses to meet with you, ask them this: *"John, I understand how busy you are, especially in these uncertain economic times, but before you make any decision, will you take just 15 minutes to listen to a CD/watch a short DVD that might give you a better idea of what it's all about?"*

If they still say no, say: *"Would it be OK if I keep in touch and keep you updated as to what's happening with the company?"*

Then every 10-12 weeks, send them any positive or exciting new information with a little post-it note saying, 'keeping you updated'. Our business is full of successful people who said no, sometimes more than once!

3. People you arrange to meet, and who don't turn up.

When this happens – and it will – you need to call the person, ask if everything is OK and tell them, in an up-beat tone, what they missed. At this point, they will probably apologise. Tell them it's OK, but you need to meet up with them a.s.a.p.

It is important that you come from a point of strength. Do not get angry, but do stress your time is valuable as well, and you would welcome a call if something comes up before your re-arranged meeting.

4. The contact does not join but gives you referrals.

There are only two ways you can increase your business: find new prospects; or obtain more contacts from the people you know.

A referral is so much more powerful than a cold call because it makes you more credible. But no one volunteers referrals; you must ask for them

5. The contact does not join, but becomes a customer.

This is a good source of referrals. Example: *"John, I have a favour to ask. With my business, my most valued resource is the customer. My priority is knowing you are happy and satisfied with your decision to be a customer. May I ask, who do you know who would be interested is saving or making money? Do you have three names that come to mind, people who would enjoy the same benefits as you?"*

6. The contact becomes a Distributor.

Another good source of referrals! Example: *"Mary, I have a favour to ask. We work our business through word of mouth. Who do you know who would like to earn more money this year than last year? Do you have three names that come to mind of people who would benefit from an extra income stream?"*

And finally: when you sign a new Distributor, remember that they will do what you do, not what you say.

Long distance

You don't need to be local to be successful. You can present the business opportunity, and build a big team, with people who are a long way away from you geographically.

As with the rest of your business, it needs attention, and consistent effort.

How to recruit and sponsor long-distance

These are the basic principles:

- Become a satisfied customer

- Contact and invite by telephone

- Send some recruiting information and/or direct people to your website

- If they are interested, explain how the money works – you can do the Martini presentation over the phone – and sign them up. They can do this online, through your website

- Get them to go to a local COP. If you cannot attend yourself, find out who is hosting the COP, and tell your new Distributor to introduce themselves to the host.

Stay in daily contact with them by phone. This is important!

- You can help them understand the business, by phone

- You can team up with your sponsor and talk them through how to do it by phone, using three-way calling

- Soon enough they will be able to do it without your help, but with the help of the other support systems (trainings, COPs, events).

If you travel to their area, get a commitment over the phone:

- To be available to meet when you are there

- Make sure they become a customer themselves

- Make sure they start their list

- Teach them how to contact and invite, how to show the Martini presentation, and how to share the benefits of the services.

Keep them exposed to the business:

- Arrange to meet them at a big event

- Conduct a three-way call with them and your active up-line

- Make sure they understand the value of massive action for the first 90 days

- Create a sense of urgency within them. What might they lose if they do not work the business?

All of this you can do at a distance, and by phone. It may appear harder at first, but get used to it and it will become natural for you.

How to explode your business

I want to share something special with you about working long-distance. It can open your team up, and boost your business more than you could have imagined.

- Teach your team to send out just one long-distance pack each week. That's a pack with a covering letter, a DVD or CD, a Sales Brochure, and an *Independence* newspaper

- Teach them to send it to an open-minded or smart person they know who lives more than 50 miles from them

- Send it Special Delivery for the greatest impact

- They must commit to sending just one pack per week. No more, no less. But they must do it. No excuses

- Teach every single person in your team to do the same

- Do it yourself: people will do what you do

- Start this habit early. Create momentum.

This method will mean that you start leveraging your team's contacts. If you have just 50 people in your team, that will be 200 long-distance packs going out every single month.

Or to put it another way, that's 2,400 packs going out every year – to people all over the UK, who your team will then teach to do the same.

Imagine the impact of that.

What it takes to succeed

Whatever you do, you need courage. Whatever course you decide upon, there is always someone to tell you you're wrong.

The tale of two lions

A Zulu warrior is teaching his sons about life. He tells them that there is a terrible battle going on inside him, a battle between two lions.

One is the Lion of courage, hope, determination, love and strength.

The other is the Lion of fear, uncertainty, worry, lethargy and doubt.

The elder son thinks about it for a moment and asks, "Which lion wins?"

The warrior replies, "The one you feed."

Say this to yourself:

> I will persist until I succeed.
>
> I was not delivered into this world in defeat.
>
> Nor does failure course in my veins.
>
> I am not a sheep waiting to be prodded by my shepherd.
>
> I am a lion and I refuse to talk, walk or sleep with the sheep.
>
> I will hear not those who weep and complain, for their disease is contagious.
>
> Let them join the sheep.
>
> The slaughterhouse of failure is not my destiny.

Say this to yourself:

Do what others won't do and you will have what others will never have.

The Impact System™

In the first part of this book, I talked about the kind of mindset you need to succeed in this business. I wanted to show how, with the right attitude, you can achieve that mindset, no matter who you are.

In the second part of this book, I have shown you how to make sure that you, as a new Distributor, start your business in the right way. You build a list of 100 plus people you know by name, and you start from there.

Follow the Impact System™, consistently, and you will succeed.

At the start of Part Two, I also showed you the power of leveraging time in building a team. I showed you how you could build a team of over 4,000 Distributors in a year.

You might think that sounds like a perfect scenario that no-one could ever achieve in reality.

But think again.

That team of over 4,000 Distributors was built on you introducing just one person each month, and on them doing the same. In other words, from each person's list of 100 people, you can build a huge business with a success rate of about one in ten.

Does that sound so hard?

Always remember that the best way to teach is by example: people will do what you do.

Follow the Impact System™, and teach the people you sponsor to follow the Impact System™ too.

The Impact System™ has been my route to success, and it can be yours too.

Now it's up to you.

Suggested reading and listening

You don't need to read all of these before you start. In fact, don't – get started!

But as you work on your business, you can keep working on yourself as well. These are some of the books and CDs I have found most useful.

Reading

Rhinoceros Success, by Scott Alexander.

How to Win Friends and Influence People, by Dale Carnegie.

Think and Grow Rich, by Napoleon Hill.

17 Secrets of the Master Prospectors, by John Kalench.

Seasons of Life, by Jim Rohn.

More Feet on the Street, by Jan Ruhe.

The Magic of Thinking Big, by David Schwartz.

Listening

The 7 Habits of Highly Effective Networkers, by Stephen Covey.

Go for No, by Richard Fenton and Andrea Waltz.

Making the shift, by Darren Hardy.

Business of the 21st Century, by Robert Kiyosaki.

The Slight Edge, by Jeff Olson.

Questions are the answers, by Allan Pease.

Building your NWM business, by Jim Rohn.

The Psychology of Winning, by Denis Waitley.

Goals; Don't just Dream it, Do it, by Chris Williams.

Don't quit

I often say there are only two ways you won't succeed at this business. One is not to join. The other is to quit. You've joined, so now make sure you don't quit.

When things go wrong, as they sometimes will,
When the road you're trudging seems all uphill,
When the funds are low and the debts are high,
And you want to smile, but you have to sigh,
When care is pressing you down a bit,
Rest if you must, but don't you quit.

Life is queer with its twists and turns,
As every one of us sometimes learns,
And many a failure turns about
When they might have won, had they stuck it out.
Don't give up though the pace seems slow,
You may succeed with another blow.

Often the struggler has given up
When he might have captured the victor's cup;
And he learned too late when the night came down,
How close he was to the golden crown.

Success is failure turned inside out
The silver tint of the clouds of doubt
And you never can tell how close you are,
It may be near when it seems so far.
So stick to the fight when you're hardest hit,
It's when things seem worst that you must not quit!